THE ILLINOIS
ThunderBolt

To: Beverly;

This was my

First book;

Larry Carli

LARRY CARLI

outskirtspress

DENVER, COLORADO

Contents

Foreword

The fearless and ruthless gladiator known as The Illinois Thunderbolt came out of the coal mines in the early 1900s to stamp himself as one of the most vicious middleweight champions of all time. Papke's four battles with Stanley Ketchel are legendary ring classics to this day.

After Ketchel's death in 1910, Papke was never universally recognized as the new champion, even though he defeated top-rated middle-weight contenders in Australia, England, and France.

Papke was vilified as a rule breaker after his second fight with Ketchel. Did he actually punch Ketchel before the start of the fight? Even though he prospered financially after his ring days were over, he could never shake his reputation of being a dirty fighter.

And finally, what caused this great champion to murder his ex-wife, and then turn the gun on himself in such a tragic fashion?

Spring Valley

LEGEND HAS IT that the Native Americans originally called this terri-
tory in Northern Illinois "the valley of the springs" due to the fact that
the hills on either side of the valley are laced with small springs that
feed into one main spring inside the valley. With all the springs and
valleys, it was easy for the early settlers to conceive the name Spring
Valley, right in the heart of Bureau County.

The environment of Spring Valley was made up of broad valleys,
wooded bluffs, fertile prairie lands, and farms. Little did the farming
residents of the 1880s realize that they were farming above the very
center of the most bituminous coalfields in the United States. The
prospecting of and discovery of coal was made in 1881 by Henry
Miller and Alexander Campbell.

Miller and Campbell bought the first coal rights in 1882 and formed
the Spring Valley Coal Company and the Spring Valley Townsite
Company in 1884. After the first shaft was put down in the ground,
Spring Valley became an instant boom town. It was called the "Magic
City" as the population rose to 3,000 in 1888 and an additional four
mines had been sunk into the ground.

Spring Valley, like any other coal town of its time, became a magnet
to just about every nationality in Europe looking for work. Spring

Valley developed a reputation as being somewhat of a lawless tough town, similar to Tombstone, Arizona, and Butte, Montana. Labor disputes and violent strikes within the coal-mining industry were common at the time.

This was the type of atmosphere that Edward Papke and his wife, the former Emma Cramer, of Brunswick, Germany, faced when they arrived. While many of the town residents worked in the coal mines, Edward went to work in the livery stable business to support his family. In 1886, Spring Valley was incorporated into a city, and the Papkes were celebrating the birth of their third son on September 17th. The Papkes named their son William Herman Papke.

The livery stable business provided for the family's basic needs of food and shelter, and Edward did not have to work in the dangerous and grimy conditions of the coal mines. Emma Papke stayed at home to take care of William Herman, or Billy, and his two older brothers, Fred and Edward. Though the town had gained a hard name, it also had a cultural side.

Spring Valley did not grow from a crossroads country store on farmhouses. It was planned with the hope it would grow to a large city. By February of 1888, two years after the incorporation of the town, two churches, two schools, a public library, and a newspaper had been established.

In 1884, Billy's sister Cora was born and became the first daughter born to Edward and Emma Papke after having three boys. In 1890, Charlotte Papke was born and became the youngest of the five Papke children. By 1891, five-year-old Billy Papke entered the Spring Valley school system and worked with his father in the livery business. Billy was raised in a strict old-fashioned German family setting where the father was the bread winner and the wife stayed home and raised the children. As a youngster, Billy was protected from the rougher elements of the city as he remained occupied with school and work.

He remained closest to his older brother Ed and followed him every-where around town. Tragedy struck the Papke family in 1899 when Billy's oldest sister Cora, a popular and pretty young teenager, died at the age of fifteen of burns she suffered when she dropped a lan-tern and caught her dress on fire. This was Billy's first encounter with death, and he would remember this for the rest of his life.

As was the custom around the early 1900s, all of the male children went to work to support the family as soon as they were old enough to do manual labor. Billy enjoyed working with his brother Ed in his father's livery stable while he was growing up, but since he had al-ready learned to read and write, it was time for him to start helping to support the family. Billy spent more time grooming and working with horses than he did at school. The Papkes were a typical hardworking middle-class family in Spring Valley that blended in well with all the other thirty-two ethnic groups living in the neighborhood.

Edward Papke was a stay-at-home family man who instilled hard-working ethics into his children's lives. He also had to be frugal with his money, and this was a habit that was impressed upon Billy from an early age. However, there was not enough money to be made in the livery business, and the only real jobs that paid well were the coal-mining jobs. Around 1902, Billy began thinking seri-ously about the coal mines, even though it was tough, grimy, and dangerous work. There had been many labor disputes in the coal mines and outright rioting between various racial groups over strike-breaking rules had occurred. The coal mines were definitely not a place for the young and timid.

Billy was athletic and shy in school and did not have much free time to play any real sports. He was basically a healthy, young, Midwestern country boy who was about to get a taste of his first real job. He did not make a lot of friends, and the majority of his free time was spent with family at home. This was all about to change.

The Coal Mines

BY 1902, BILLY was sixteen years old and had developed a powerful physique. He liked working with the family in the livery stable, but the coal mines paid more money, and he saw a lot of early model flashy cars around town that he would like to own someday. The Spring Valley Coal Company had over 2,000 employees by 1905 and had undergone some violent labor-related strikes. The coal-mining company had brought in strike breakers to break up the unions, and this escalated into race-related riots. First, the Italian immigrants were brought in as strike breakers, and then when that failed to break up the unions, the blacks were brought in as scabs, or strike breakers. These strike-breaking issues caused rioting between the blacks and Italians and the other ethnic groups working in the mines.

Billy would find the mines a much tougher place to work than the livery business. It was during a lockout that Billy gained his employment in the mines. Many of the miners for pure pleasure held bare-knuckle tough man contests between them. A winner was usually declared when one of the combatants was knocked unconscious on the ground and was unable to get up.

It was not long before the other miners took note of the young, tough, blond-haired German youth with the pompadour haircut. After knocking out a string of local miners, Billy had gained a reputation as "king of the tough man contests." He did not just outbox the other miners; he knocked them cold with his left hook.

Billy grew to about five feet nine inches tall and weighed a solid 155 pounds. He had broad shoulders, huge, powerful forearms, and a small waist, giving his upper torso a V-shaped appearance. Billy knocked out miners over six feet tall, and over 200 hundred pounds, since there were no weight limits in these contests.

Billy made a lot of money on side bets, and he had to explain to his mother when he came home from work, why he had bruises on his face and skinned knuckles. Older brother Ed knew what was going on and said nothing to the family, developing a bond between the two brothers.

Billy's reputation spread throughout Bureau County and the broad-shouldered teenager was ready to fight anyone if the money was right. He was often called a kraut or other uncomplimentary remarks by other coal miners, who eventually lived to regret their remarks. After work, Billy would frequent the local gyms and took a liking to the aggressive style of boxing of Bantamweight and Featherweight Champion Terry McGovern. McGovern had a habit of coming out at the first bell and throwing wild punches in an attempt to knock out his opponents as fast as possible. Billy would read all he could about McGovern and copied his style of fighting when knocking out the other coal miners.

Billy's reputation as a young fearsome warrior spread throughout the Midwest mining camps. One day, famous East Coast boxing manager and promoter Tom E. Jones showed up at a local gym in Spring Valley to watch Billy work out. Jones saw the incredible power and stamina that the youngster possessed and suspected he had a future champion in his midst.

Jones showed Billy how to improve his footwork and cut off the ring on an opponent. Billy was a fast learner and spent hours in the gym perfecting his craft.

Billy's parents did not want him to be a prizefighter, but at the age of nineteen, Billy had already made up his mind that the big money was in fighting and not in working in the coal mines. While working out and waiting to turn pro, he was breaking the ribs of opponents during sparring sessions with his vicious body punching and inside uppercuts.

In retrospect, turning to professional boxing in 1905 may have been a very wise move for Billy Papke. Around this time, some of the most vicious and deadly labor battles occurred between union and nonunion miners. Around 1909, the Cherry mine disaster occurred where close to 300 miners died in an underground explosion. It was the largest mine disaster in Illinois history. While Billy was becoming middleweight champion of the world, many of his fellow workers and friends suffered a horrible death.

The Illinois Thunderbolt

AT THE AGE of nineteen, on November 5, 1905, Billy made his professional debut in New York City. He fought a six-round draw with Battling Hurley. Billy pounded Hurley at will, however, no decision was rendered unless a knockout occurred. Two weeks later, Jones took Billy to Boston where he fought a twenty-round draw with Dave Deschler. Billy showed incredible stamina and dominated the fight but was unable to knock Deschler out.

Billy fought for the first time in 1906 in Illinois and won a four-round decision over the very scared Mexican Wonder in LaSalle. For this fight, Billy received a grand total of five dollars. Billy returned to LaSalle a month later and registered his first knockout when he stopped Red Morrisey in three rounds.

Fighting once a month on a continual basis, Billy was in the ring again in LaSalle in June and knocked out Buster Teegan with a vicious three-punch combination all to the body. Billy was developing quite a reputation as a vicious body puncher, and he patterned his aggressive style of fighting after his hero, world Bantamweight and Featherweight Boxing Champion Terry McGovern. Papke would allow his opponents to come to him, and then he would counter punch with vicious punches to the head and body. Papke also developed a vicious short corkscrew uppercut which he would throw at close quarters in a fight.

After knocking out Jack Denny in one round, Billy stepped into the ring in July for his first ten-round main event in Illinois. Billy gave the more experienced Carl Purdy a vicious body beating and stopped him in the seventh round in LaSalle. Billy celebrated his twentieth birthday in September and took a three-month break from the ring. He returned to the ring in November and knocked out an over matched Milt Kinney in three rounds in Peoria and stopped the tough Kid Farmer in the same ring in six rounds.

At this point, after registering six knockouts among his seven wins, Billy felt secure enough in his boxing abilities to stop working in the coal mines of Spring Valley. Billy moved with his brother Ed to Kewanee, Illinois, around January of 1907 and fought twice that month. He knocked out Tommy Wallace in three rounds on January 15th, and returned two weeks later to win a ten-round decision over Dick Fitzpatrick in Peoria.

Tom Jones was beginning to realize that he had, indeed, the makings of a future champion in Billy Papke with his incredible power and stamina. Billy had knockout power in both fists and could fight all day long at a rapid pace. In February, Jones brought Billy back to his birthplace of Spring Valley to show his hometown fans how much he had improved in the ring. Billy flattened Carl Anderson within the first minute of the fight. Anderson had to be helped, still in a groggy mental state, from the ring. In March, Billy was back in the ring in Peoria to fight another unbeaten fighter in Billy Rhodes. In the battle of unbeaten fighters, Billy took an easy unanimous decision to stay unbeaten.

Rhodes demanded a rematch, and Billy was held to a ten-round draw in Davenport, Iowa, on March 26th. In April, Billy knocked out Johnny Carroll in four rounds, and in May, he was matched with his first world-ranked opponent in Tough Tony Caponi.

The Caponi match was to be held in Davenport, Iowa, where Billy felt he had been robbed of a decision in his rematch with Billy Rhodes. Billy still went through with the match, as he felt that a win would qualify him as a serious contender for the middleweight title. Billy held Caponi to a ten-round draw in a very tough and competitive fight. After the fight, Caponi agreed to fight Billy in a rematch in Spring Valley. Billy tuned up for the rematch by knocking out Jack Morgan in Peoria in seven rounds in June, and followed up with a knockout win two weeks later of Foster Walker in two rounds in Detroit, Michigan.

Just prior to the rematch, Caponi refused to go through with the fight unless the fight was called a draw if both men were standing at the end of ten rounds. Billy agreed to the terms and the rematch was held on June 20th. Billy battered Caponi all over the ring and won nine out of the ten rounds on the newspaper's scorecards. Unfortunately, Billy was unable to stop Caponi, and the match was ruled a draw.

Billy returned to the ring in September and knocked out Tommy Sullivan in three rounds in Methuen, Massachusetts, and Terry Martin two weeks later in three rounds in Philadelphia, Pennsylvania. Billy turned twenty-one years of age right after the Martin fight, and he continued on his winning ways by knocking out Cy Flynn in three rounds in Brazil, Indiana. After this win, Billy was elated to find out that his manager, Tom Jones, was able to lure Tony Caponi back into the ring for a third match on November 14th, in Peoria. Billy tuned up for the Caponi rematch by winning an easy six-round decision over Pat O'Keefe in Philadelphia on November 9th.

Caponi took the Papke rematch because the winner of the fight was promised a shot at top-ranked middleweight contender Hugo Kelly. Caponi entered the ring very confident that his experience would eventually overcome the raw power of Papke.

Billy fought an absolutely disciplined fight as he blasted Caponi out in the second round to leave no doubt as to who was the better fighter.

Billy was now promised a shot at top-ranked contender Hugo Kelly. The Kelly fight was set for December 30th, with the winner promised a shot at middleweight champion Stanley Ketchel.

Billy had become the toast of the Midwest boxing circles, and local Kewanee sportswriter Bing Johnson labeled him the Illinois Thunderbolt due to his whirlwind style of fighting. Billy lived up to his nickname by tuning up for the Kelly fight by taking on two opponents in one night in Chelsea, Massachusetts, on November 22nd. Billy knocked out Charlie Haghey in one round in the first fight, and then returned later in the same evening to knock out Bartley Connolly in four rounds.

The fight with Hugo Kelly was to take place in Milwaukee, Wisconsin. Kelly had a reputation of knocking off other top-rated fighters. Kelly's real name was Ugo Micheli, and he was born in Florence, Italy. Kelly came to the United States as a youngster and settled in the Chicago area. He took Kelly as a last name to obtain a solid Irish following, and his aggressive style of fighting was a favorite with the fans. Kelly had already defeated such top rated fighters as Jack (Twin) Sullivan and Philadelphia Jack O'Brien. Kelly had been promised a title fight with Ketchel if he defeated Papke, and he was not about to lose this fight.

On the evening of December 30, both fighters stepped into the ring at Schlitz Park in Milwaukee to do battle. The fight was fought at a fierce pace with both fighters rocking each other with solid blows numerous times during the fight. At the end of ten rounds, the newspaper writers felt that Papke had earned a close decision, but the official verdict was a draw. Stanley Ketchel immediately stated that he would only fight Papke or Kelly if there was a clear winner in a rematch.

The rematch was to take place on March 16, 1908, at the Hippodrome in Milwaukee. Even though Stanley Ketchel was the recognized world middleweight champion, the Papke-Kelly rematch was billed as a fight for the American middleweight championship. Billy tuned up for this fight by knocking out unbeaten Walter Stanton in four rounds in Boston on January 21st.

Papke and Kelly stepped into the ring at the Hippodrome on March 16th, with the winner getting a promised shot at Ketchel. The bell rang for the opening round and the fighters started at a fierce pace. On this particular night, Papke was a human punching machine, fighting nonstop for the whole fight and hitting Kelly with vicious head and body shots for all ten rounds. A badly beaten and bloodied Kelly barely made it to the final bell. This time, there was no doubt about the outcome as Billy was awarded a popular unanimous decision with the crowd.

The Illinois Thunderbolt had arrived, and the only thing that stood between him and the middleweight championship was a man named Stanley Ketchel. Billy was unbeaten in twenty-nine fights over a three year period, and he felt that there was no man that he could not beat, including Stanley Ketchel. He now waited for Ketchel to agree to the fight.

Stanley Ketchel

STANLEY KETCHEL WAS born Stanislaus Kiecal on September 14, 1886, in Grand Rapids, Michigan. Born just three days before Billy Papke, he was similar in build, around five feet nine, and around 155 pounds of pure lean muscle. He began his professional boxing career in 1903 in Butte, Montana, and changed his name to Stanley Ketchel on the advice of his manager Joe O'Conner. O'Conner felt that the name change would draw more crowds of miners to his fights in his adopted hometown of Butte.

As a youngster, Ketchel had lived a bohemian lifestyle, leaving his Michigan home around the age of fifteen and riding the rails through Canada and the Midwest. Ketchel eventually settled in Butte, which was somewhat of a lawless and rough-and-tumble copper mining town.

Ketchel gained employment as a bouncer in the local saloons, and his reputation quickly spread among the locals as a man with a mean disposition and a deadly right-hand punch. After knocking out several miners close to twice his size, he was encouraged to try professional boxing by the local promoters.

Ketchel was what was called a natural-born fighter, with his killer instinct and deadly right-hand punch. He was aggressive and was always willing to take several punches just to land one of his hay-makers. He never learned the true art of scientific boxing, as evidenced by his two decision losses to Maurice Thompson early in his professional career.

With more experience, Ketchel became an unbeatable force in the ring, knocking out everybody in sight in his first few years as a professional. In September of 1907, he was matched with Joe Thomas in a fight for the vacant middleweight title. Ketchel knocked Thomas out in the twenty-second round to claim the title, and beat Thomas handily in a twenty-round rematch in December.

In February of 1908, Ketchel knocked out Mike (Twin) Sullivan in one round, and his brother Jack (Twin) Sullivan in twenty rounds in May at Colma, California. Now, only Billy Papke stood in his way for universal championship recognition.

The Ketchel-Papke match was to be a ten-round non-title fight scheduled for June 4th in the Hippodrome in Milwaukee. Papke tuned up for the fight by taking on Eddie McGoorty on May 31st in a six-round exhibition match in Kenosha, Wisconsin.

Local promoters released a story that Papke actually visited Ketchel at his training camp prior to the fight. Supposedly, the two fighters exchanged greetings and both predicted victories for themselves. Ketchel advised Papke that he had seen his last fight with Hugo Kelly and was looking forward to having a tough fight. Papke advised that he would be ready to give Ketchel all that he could handle in the upcoming fight.

On June 4th, both fighters stepped into the ring with the odds favoring Ketchel ten to seven to win. Ketchel was wearing his long baggy grey pants, and Papke was in his usual black jockstrap. Even though both fighters were listed at the same height and weight, Ketchel appeared to be slightly the taller of the two. The referee called the fighters to the center of the ring and gave them their prefight instructions.

The fighters returned to their corners, and Papke's manager, Tom Jones, advised him to watch out for Ketchel coming out fast and trying to land a damaging blow before he could get set. Jones had seen Ketchel catch several other fighters off guard at the beginning of several of his fights. The bell rang for round one, and Papke immediately ignored Jones' advice by walking to ring center and touching gloves with Ketchel. Ketchel immediately tapped his glove with his left hand . . . and drove a straight right-hand cross to Papke's forehead. Papke stumbled halfway across the ring before landing on the seat of his pants. He arose in a dazed condition and took a vicious pounding throughout the first round. Papke's great conditioning allowed him to finish the round, but he returned to his corner with a chipped tooth and swollen face.

Papke answered the bell for round two but was not completely recovered from the first-round pounding. Ketchel continued to pound Papke with both hands in the second and third rounds but was unable to put him away. Papke slowly worked his way back into the fight and actually dropped Ketchel in the fourth round with a right-hand uppercut as Ketchel was boring inside. By the sixth round, the fighters were battling on even terms, and the crowd of 5,000 people in the Hippodrome were on their feet cheering the action. The fighters fought nonstop for the rest of the fight, with Papke actually winning several of the last few rounds. At the final bell, the fighters had to be separated, and the crowd gave both fighters a standing ovation.

The referee raised Ketchel's hand at the end of the fight and few people in the fight crowd disagreed with the decision. Both fighters showed respect for each other and spoke in the ring after the fight. Papke's manager, Tom Jones, went to Ketchel's dressing room after the fight and asked for a rematch with the title on the line. Ketchel's manager, Joe O'Connor, agreed to a title match, but insisted on a twenty-five-round fight.

While manager Tom Jones was trying to arrange the title match, Billy kept busy by boxing a six-round exhibition in his hometown of Kewanee on July 4th, and took on two fighters in one night on August 13th in Boston. In the first fight, Billy knocked out Johnny Carroll in two rounds, and then returned later the same evening to stop world-ranked contender Frank Mantell in the first round. On August 18th, Billy slapped Sailor Burke around the ring in a six-round exhibition match in New York.

Billy returned to Kewanee and learned that his title fight with Ketchel was scheduled for September 7th in Los Angeles, California. The fight was to be scheduled for twenty-five rounds and former heavyweight champion Jim Jeffries was to be the referee. Billy trained diligently for the fight in Kewanee, and this time remembered what his manager had told him just before the start of the Ketchel fight in Milwaukee.

Call Me Champ

BILLY CLOSED HIMSELF off from family and friends as he trained on a daily basis like a demon. He realized to win the title, he would probably have to knock Ketchel out, as the rule of the day was that if a champion was still standing at the end of the fight, it was very unlikely that the title would change hands.

The fight was going to be held on the Labor Day holiday, and the arena in Los Angeles was sure to be packed. This fight was probably the biggest fight in the country at the time. Sportswriters and famous fighters from around the world would be at this fight. The fight crowd was abuzz about the last fight and how the blond gladiator Papke had stood up to the great Stanley Ketchel.

Ketchel advised the press that he wanted this fight more than Papke because he wanted to prove to the world that he was not in top shape for the last fight and took Papke lightly. Ketchel vowed to knock Papke out to end the controversy over who was the best middleweight fighter in the world. Ketchel promised the sportswriters that the kraut would not be standing at the end of the fight.

As was customary, both Tom Jones and Joe O'Conner predicted victories for their fighters and approved of former heavyweight champion Jim Jeffries as the referee for the contest. Based upon their first fight,

Ketchel was considered the favorite in the rematch of odds from eight to five to two to one.

On September 7th, both gladiators stepped into the ring in Los Angeles to do battle and settle the dispute as to who was the better man. Referee Jeffries was also in the ring and the fighters struck several poses for the news media and cameras. Ketchel was wearing his favorite grey baggy trunks, and Papke, as usual, clad only in his famous black jockstrap. Both fighters appeared to be in perfect condition, with Ketchel joking and laughing with Jeffries and the sportswriters at ringside. Papke, in sharp contrast, was very serious, and kept looking down at the floor. Eventually, the picture taking was completed, and Jeffries called the fighters to ring center to give them their prefight instructions. Papke appeared to be preoccupied at ring center and upon completion of the instructions, both fighters returned to their corner to await the first bell.

The bell rang, and both fighters walked toward ring center. Papke, remembering the first fight, did not shake hands and missed with a wild right hand at ring center. Ketchel landed the first punch of the fight, a light left to the face. During the first real exchange of the fight, Billy beat Ketchel to the punch, landing a sharp left and right combination that knocked Ketchel flat on his back. He arose with a surprised look on his face, with one eye partially closed, and bleeding from the mouth. Papke attacked wildly with uppercuts and hooks and rained blows on Ketchel from all angles. Ketchel had been knocked down a total of five times before he was saved by the bell in the first round. Ketchel staggered back to his corner with the injured eye completely closed and a fountain of blood running from his broken nose.

To the surprise of many in the crowd, Ketchel answered the bell for the second round to continue the battle. Papke came out for the second round, ripping vicious uppercuts to Ketchel's face and body. Ketchel's face was a bloody mess, but he fought back with wild swings which did not carry much power. Papke dropped Ketchel to his knees with one solid right uppercut, but Ketchel gamely arose to fight on. Ketchel was being severely hammered in a corner when the bell rang, ending the round.

The onslaught continued as Papke kept after Ketchel, never giving him a chance to rest. Ketchel showed great courage in surviving the first two rounds, but Papke also appeared to have punched himself out in trying for the early knockout. Ketchel's mouth was a mess with a steady stream of blood flowing down and one eye closed. He fought back gamely, but his punches seemed to have no effect on Papke. Only Ketchel's will to survive kept him in the fight.

By the eighth round, Papke was landing at will, and by modern-day standards, the fight would have been stopped at this point. Ketchel refused to give up, however, and wished to fight on until he either won by knockout or was knocked out. Referee Jeffries allowed the fighters to battle without much interruption. Jeffries, a former heavyweight champion, was used to the sight of blood, and he allowed the fight to continue as long as Ketchel wanted to fight.

By the tenth round, Papke had caught his second wind and made a serious attempt to end the fight as he hammered Ketchel with both fists to head and body. By this point, Ketchel could barely see out of the other eye. It appeared to ringsiders and the crowd that Papke actually seemed to enjoy torturing Ketchel with left hooks and right uppercuts to the head and body as he had a perpetual smile on his face.

Ketchel answered the bell for the eleventh round and was swinging blindly at Papke and was missing his target by a foot. Papke, with Ketchel's blood smeared all over his arms and shoulders, would continue to bore in close after Ketchel with vicious uppercuts as the crowd started to holler at Referee Jeffries to stop the fight. Toward the end of the round, a right hand knocked Ketchel completely out of the ring. Ketchel was pushed back into the ring by the sportswriters at ringside, as was the case when Jack Dempsey was knocked out of the ring by Luis Firpo in a 1923 heavyweight title fight. The bell rang, ending the eleventh round as Ketchel got back into the ring at the count of nine.

Ketchel literally stumbled out to ring center for the twelfth round, only able to see shadows. Papke immediately dropped him with a right hand, but Ketchel actually beat the count. A second straight right hand put Ketchel down in ring center. He was too weak to arise and was counted out in a sitting position staring at his corner. If ever a man went out to defeat on his shield, it was Stanley Ketchel. In the other corner, Billy Papke was enjoying the rewards of being the new middleweight champion of the world.

After the fight, Ketchel lay down on his dressing room table and looked like he had been in a war. One eye was totally closed, and the other was rapidly closing. His nose was broken, lips were cut to shreds, and he had lumps and bruises all over his face. He claimed that he let Papke get the jump on him in the first round, and it was an uphill battle from then on. Ketchel had no complaints about the fight, but insisted he was sure he would regain his title in a rematch. Ketchel's trainer, Pete (the Goat) Stone, on the other hand, was livid and told everyone that he felt that Papke took advantage of Ketchel before he was set to fight in the first round.

Papke, in the other dressing room, was jubilant and unscathed. He stated that he had won fair and square. He told all the reporters that he was not going to fall for Ketchel's habit of tapping gloves and then landing a sneak punch, as was the case in what he called "the Milwaukee double cross." Papke said that he merely beat Ketchel to the punch, as Ketchel had done to him in the first fight. Papke said that he was returning to Kewanee to rest, and then buy the biggest and fastest car that he could find. He told reporters that he had developed a passion for fast cars, and with the money he earned, he could now afford to buy his dream car, and some real estate in his hometown.

BILLY PAPKE, Kewanee's Middleweight World Champion (1908-09) pictured with his Kewanee supporters. Front, from left, Papke's manager Tom Jones, who also managed Heavyweight Champion Jess Willard, Walt Parlier, Papke, Buck Neward, and Cully Faulkner. Middle, from left, Art Lundine, Hugh Hill, George Cullenbine, Dinny O'Donnell and Al King. In back are Ed Moran and John P. Brady. (Picture donated by C.U. Verstraete and Herb Kuster.)

BILLY PAPKE AND HIS FRIENDS.

SOME SPORTING MEN OF KEWANEE, ILL., WHO WILL BACK THIS AMBITIOUS BOXER AGAINST ANY MIDDLEWEIGHT IN THE COUNTRY FOR $5,000 T. E. JONES IS HIS MANAGER.

Billy Papke residence in Kewanee, Illinois. Photo by Larry Lock

SCHUTTE/POWELL
BOXING ARCHIVES

BILLY PAPKE

Billy Papke boxing card

Billy Papke in early boxing career

PAPKE JEFFRIES KETCHEL

Vernon Arena – Labor Day 1908

Photo taken prior to second Ketchel-Papke fight

Here you see Ketchel's swollen left eye. His right eye was a carbon copy. Papke's arm and back was smeared with Ketchel blood. All because the "Protect Yourself At All Times"—"Come Out Fighting" Rule had not yet made its appearance.

Ketchel-Papke second fight

Ketchel lost the middleweight title to Billy Papke in September 1908. (The referee is former heavyweight champion Jim Jeffries.) In all, "The Michigan Assassin" beat Papke in three of their four bouts. Their rivalry is among the greatest in ring history.

Papke knocks Ketchel out of ring eleventh round, second fight

Papke takes the championship as Ketchel takes the
full count in twelfth round

Ring Legends

CHAMP MEETS EX-CHAMP—Kewanee's Billy Papke left) and James J. Jeffries, onetime heavyweight champion, pose at Vernon, Calif., near Los Angeles after Papke had knocked out Stanley Ketchel in the 12th round to win the world's middleweight championship on Labor Day, 1908. Jeffries refereed the match. This picture was sent by Papke to Hugh Hill, in Kewanee. Hill was a druggist here for many years.

Billy and brother Ed celebrate championship in Billy's new car

Billy Papke Champion middleweight of the world.

Ed. Papke manager.

Billy Papke, the new champion

Stanley Ketchel regains the middleweight title by eleventh round knockout in their rematch on Thanksgiving Day, 1908

GETTING INTO PROPER CONDITION IN THE BUSY TRAINING CAMP BEFORE THE LAST BATTLE WITH STANLEY KETCHELL.

BILLY PAPKE, ONE OF THE BEST.

MANY BELIEVE HE WILL PUT KETCHELL AWAY IF THEY EVER COME TOGETHER AGAIN.

Lull Before The Storm

Papke In Bad At Paris

Assaults Dan McKettrick, Manager of Willie Lewis, During
Recent Boxing Show

Edna Pulver-Papke

Ed Papke on left and Billy Papke on right

Billy Papke on the left and brother Ed Papke sailing to Europe, circa 1911

Advertisement for Sullivan v. Papke fight in London, England

A scene in the Papke-Sullivan fight in London. The Britisher was knocked out in the ninth round

Papke knocks out Sullivan in ninth round to gain British version of middleweight title

Papke weighs in nude to make weight for Georges Carpentier fight,
Paris, France, circa 1912

WHEN BILLY PAPKE FOUGHT BERNARD IN PARIS.
THE AMERICAN MIDDLEWEIGHT HANDLED THE FRENCHMAN WITH APPARENT EASE—HERE HE IS SHOWN
BLOCKING AND JABBING, WHILE THE REFEREE SEEMS TO BE GETTING ANXIOUS.

BERNARD DROPPED WITH A PAPKE PUNCH.
THIS TOOK PLACE IN THE SIXTH ROUND; HE MANAGED TO GET TO HIS FEET, BUT WAS IMMEDIATELY FLOORED
AGAIN, AND THE SECOND TIME HE STAYED DOWN FOR THE FULL COUNT.

Billy Papke (above) knocks out George Bernard in their title fight
in Paris on December 4, 1912. It was Billy's last successful title
defense before losing the crown to Frank Klaus.   Int'l Boxing

Billy Papke defends French version of middleweight title by knocking
out George Bernard in seven rounds, circa 1912

REGISTRATION CARD 3723 No. 194

1 Name in full William H. Papke 30

2 Kewanee Ill

3 Date of birth 17 Sept 1886

4 Natural Born Citizen

5 Spring Valley Ill. U.S.A.

6

7 Truck Farmer

8 Self

Kewanee

9 Wife and Three Children

10 Married Caucasian

11

12 Dependent Wife and Children

I affirm that I have verified above answers and that they are true.

3723 W H Papke

Billy Papke's draft card, circa 1917, Kewanee, Illinois

Billy Papke meets middleweight champion Harry Greb
(on right), circa 1925

Billy Papke makes debut as referee in Pasadena, California, circa 1926

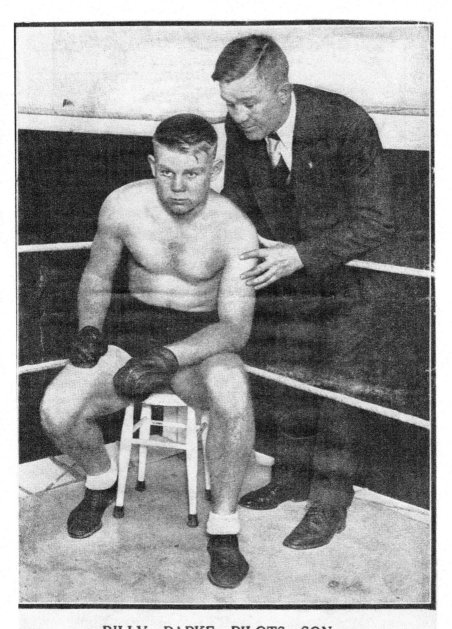

BILLY PAPKE PILOTS SON.

FORMER MIDDLEWEIGHT CHAMPION IN "JUNIOR'S" CORNER, AS
BOY, A LIGHT-HEAVY, AWAITS BATTLE GONG.

Papkes—Both of 'Em

A quarter of a century ago Billy Papke of Kewanee, Ill., was one of the leading middleweight fighters on the Pacific coast and a champion for a time. Now he is in San Francisco again, this time with Billy Papke Jr., a boy of 19, who will appear on a huge boxing program. Photo shows (left to right) Billy Papke and Billy Papke Jr.

Billy Papke with Billy Papke Jr. Circa 1932

2015 photo of 216 Ruby Ave, Balboa Island Section of Newport Beach, California, site of murder-suicide, Thanksgiving Day, 1936.
Photos by Michael Valentini

Champion No More

BILLY RETURNED TO Kewanee a hero. He was given a rousing welcome in the Boiler Works town. He was met with brass bands that turned out to meet him upon his train arrival in town. Billy was paraded through the streets, and a crowd of hundreds were on hand to salute him as he motored down the streets. Billy was accompanied by his father, brother Ed, and manager, Tom E. Jones.

Billy and Tom Jones gave emotional speeches about how thrilled they were to receive the fantastic support from the hometown fans. Billy came out of the Ketchel fight with hardly a scratch and said that he was willing to take on all comers for his title. Tom Jones reminded the crowd that the first title defense was to be a rematch with Hugo Kelly in October at the Hippodrome in Milwaukee.

Billy celebrated his twenty-second birthday on September 17th by purchasing a brand-new special model Stutz roadster, green in color. Billy, remembering his father's advice to always save and invest his money, bought a home and chicken farm in his adopted hometown of Kewanee. Billy would reside at 300 Roosevelt Avenue while living in Kewanee. He received $6,600 from the Ketchel fight and enjoyed touring the Midwest and East Coast in his new roadster and did not worry too much about his rematch with Hugo Kelly.

Billy was not as charismatic as Stanley Ketchel and did not drink and attend all-night parties as such boxing heroes as former heavyweight champion John L. Sullivan had done in the past. The sportswriters of the day loved to write about Stanley Ketchel and followed his every move. Ketchel would give the sportswriters plenty of stories to write about, some true, and some not so true.

Billy began training for the Kelly fight and felt confident that he could beat him again in Milwaukee. One week prior to the scheduled fight, the state of Wisconsin advised that they would only allow boxing exhibitions and would not allow any title fight to be held in their state. The prior Kelly fight had been advertised as an exhibition, but the local boxing officials were now wise as to the fact that the rematch was more than just a boxing exhibition. Billy returned to Kewanee and stopped training. Toward the end of October, Tom Jones advised him that he had signed for him to defend his title against Ketchel on Thanksgiving Day in California. Billy was caught by surprise by the switch in opponents, and his friends asked Jones to reschedule the fight to a later date to give Billy more time to prepare for the fight. Jones would not listen to any talk about rescheduling the match as he stated that the fight had already been set with the California promoters.

In California, just days before the Ketchel match, and not in fighting shape, Papke had a major dispute with Jones about his share of the purse. Billy became even more suspicious of his manager when the fight was moved at the last minute just outside of the San Francisco city limits.

Billy stepped into the ring, both physically and mentally unprepared for the fight. He appeared nervous prior to the start of a contest for the first time in his career. The bell rang, and Ketchel tore into him in the first round. Billy staggered and wobbled several times. This fight was all Ketchel's as he battered Papke at will with a vicious body attack that would have caused most men to quit around the end of the seventh round. Papke and Ketchel were very similar fighters, where neither one of them would ever quit in a fight. They would continue on until counted out. Papke came out every round trying to make a fight of it, but Ketchel continually beat him to the punch in every round. During the eleventh round, Billy was knocked flat on his back by a Ketchel right hand near the ropes. He attempted to rise, but he did not beat the ten count. Billy would later claim that he could not hear the whole count due to the crowd noise, but he appeared to be a thoroughly beaten fighter regardless.

This would be the only time in his career that he was ever stopped in a fight. He made no excuses for his loss to the press and immediately split with his manager, Tom Jones, after the fight. He collected another $6,600 for the fight, which was below the expected $8,000 for his share of the purse. Billy's brother Ed would take over as trainer/manager after this fight.

There would be no parade for Billy when he returned home this time. Kewanee sport fans were shocked by Billy's loss. This was the first time that a middleweight champion had ever regained his title. Many Kewanee fans lost a lot of money betting on the fight and refused to believe that Billy could have been so dominated by Ketchel.

National sportswriters would write that Billy was so beat up in this fight that his wife did not even recognize him when he came home. The truth was, however, that Billy was not even married until 1910. Billy was also in good enough shape to fight Hugo Kelly to a twenty-five-round draw in Los Angeles just twenty days after the Ketchel fight.

Billy had made close to $100,000 in his first three years of boxing, which would make him an easy millionaire by today's standards. He took a fight in Los Angeles against Fireman Jim Flynn and looked very lackadaisical in losing a ten-round newspaper decision. Billy obtained the services of Sam Berger and Al Lippe as replacements for Tom Jones, and it was announced that Stanley Ketchel was willing to give Billy a rematch if he would beat Hugo Kelly again. The Papke-Kelly title eliminator match was set for May in Colma, California. At the first bell in the rematch, Papke tore into Kelly and dropped him with a straight right to the head. Kelly arose with a large cut over his right eye. Billy went right after Kelly and knocked him down and out with a series of vicious body blows. Kelly never made it past the first minute of the fight and had to be helped to his dressing room.

The rematch with Stanley Ketchel for the middleweight title was set for July 5th, in the same ring in Colma. Billy went into serious training for the fight in Kewanee to prepare for the rematch. This was to be the fight to determine once and for all who the better man was in the ring. Billy returned to California a couple of weeks before the fight to finish his training.

Billy stepped into the ring on July 5th in the best shape of his life. Movie cameras were at ringside to film the fight, and Billy can be seen inside the ring wearing his customary jockstrap with extremely tan arms and legs. Ketchel is in his customary dark-colored baggy trunks, and the referee is Billy Roche.

Both fighters came out for the first round and began fighting without shaking hands. Both fighters chose to fight on the inside, and neither fighter took a backward step the whole first round. This vicious in-fighting set the pattern of the fight, round after round. Neither fighter would take a backward step, and Ketchel appeared to get the better of the exchanges during the first half of the fight. Both fighters can be seen to hit on the break, elbow, and sneak in punches at every opportunity. During the second half of the fight, Papke appears to come on and get the better of the vicious exchanges. Both fighters are content to just to blast away at each other on the inside with no regard for defense. Both fighters appear to be blood smeared, and they had to be separated as they continued to fight after the final bell. This was a classic fight between two great fighters.

After the fight concluded, Billy Roche went to Ketchel's corner and raised his hand as the winner of the fight. This decision brought howls of protest from the Papke backers in the crowd, and cheers from Ketchel's fans. The fight was very close, and either man could have been declared the winner. Since the fight was very close, most boxing writers agreed that it was difficult to take the title away from Ketchel.

Billy felt that he should have received no less than a draw in the fight, and several hometown newspapers back in the Kewanee area claimed that he was robbed of the decision by the referee Billy Roche. Incredibly, only nine days later, Billy would step into the ring again in Los Angeles and fight a ten-round, no-decision match with Fireman Jim Flynn. Billy would finish out the year with a six-round decision win over Willie Lewis in October in Philadelphia, and lose a six-round decision to clever Frank Klaus in Pittsburgh in November.

Stanley Ketchel had been knocked out by Jack Johnson in twelve rounds in October of 1909 in a fight for the heavyweight title. Since the knockout, rumors had been floating around that Ketchel was retiring and was going to vacate his middleweight title. Ed Papke had made arrangements with French promoters for Billy to meet Willie Lewis in a bout that would be advertised for the middleweight title.

Billy and Ed sailed to France, where Billy immediately fell into disfavor with the French press. While attending a boxing fundraiser before the fight with Lewis and his manager Dan McKetrick, a comment was made that Stanley Ketchel was the real middleweight champion. Papke, thinking that McKetrick made the comment, punched the diminutive manager in the jaw without provocation. This led to Papke making a quick exit on the run from the fundraiser to escape the wrath of the crowd of sportswriters and boxing officials.

On March 19th, Billy stepped into a Paris ring with the crowd 100 percent behind Willie Lewis to win the match. Billy looked much bigger than Lewis inside of the ring. Billy, taking no chance on a decision or a disqualification, went after Lewis from the first bell, landing vicious punches to the head. Papke did virtually no body work and knocked Lewis out with his familiar right uppercut and left hook to the head in the third round. After the match, Papke was declared the winner midst a chorus of boos from the crowd. Papke claimed the middleweight title and the French press begged any fighter to come to France to defeat the vilified Papke.

Billy returned to the States and defended his claim to the title by knocking out perennial contender Joe Thomas in sixteen rounds in May in San Francisco. Billy carried Thomas for the first fifteen rounds until the crowd started booing for lack of action. Billy responded to the crowd's shouts for more action and stopped Thomas easily in the following round. Billy then won a twelve-round decision over Jack (Twin) Sullivan in June in Boston. Billy dropped Sullivan during the match and gave him a vicious body beating. Sullivan tried to claim foul during the match, but his claims were denied by the referee.

After taking five months off from the ring after his knockout at the hands of Jack Johnson, Ketchel decided to return to the ring after hearing that Billy Papke was claiming his title. During the first part of 1910, Ketchel fought a series of non-title fights with Sam Langford, Frank Klaus, Willie Lewis, and Jim Smith. Most of these fights were no-decision exhibitions as he was working himself back into fighting shape. However, fate would intervene in October of 1910, and Stanley Ketchel would never fight again.

Billy Takes a Bride

THE NEWS COMING out of the Kewanee newspapers on July 21st, 1910, was shocking. The headlines read: "BILLY PAPKE WEDS AND QUITS PUGILISTIC RING." Billy Papke sent the following telegram to his brother Ed from Buffalo, New York. "Well, Ed, the big show is over. Signed Bill and Edna."

The bride's name was Edna E. Pulver, and she was the daughter of a wealthy manufacturer from Hamilton-Ontario, Canada. The pretty twenty-year-old dark-haired socialite apparently had met Billy in New York during one of his East Coast tour of fights in the preceding years. The news of the marriage explained why during many of his trips to the East Coast he took a roundabout route through Canada on the way to New York in his flashy roadster.

The young couple fell in love, and when Edna's parents planned a three-month voyage to Europe for the whole family, Billy decided it was time for him to make the commitment. Just as Edna's parents were preparing to leave, she decided to jump into Billy's roadster and make the trip to Buffalo, New York, for the wedding. The couple stayed in New York City for the honeymoon, and after a couple of weeks, they motored to Kewanee where they planned to live. Edna's parents continued on to Europe without her in a rather shocked state, to say the least.

Billy was financially secure with over a hundred thousand dollars in his bank account, and he and his wife were given a royal welcome by the local townspeople on their return to Kewanee. The young couple was very popular with the local crowd, Billy with his blond hair and athletic build, and Edna with her dark hair, pretty face, and cultured social graces. They were frequently seen motoring around town in Billy's new Glide touring car, and they always had time to stop and say hello to all their friends.

Billy had invested wisely in local real estate, which included buying a home and a chicken farm on the outskirts of town. He told everyone that he was financially secure and that he did not need to fight anymore. It was not clear if it was really Billy's idea to quit the ring, or Edna's idea.

Billy took to farming and was glad he had retired from the coal mines after hearing about the recent Cherry coal-mining disaster near his birthplace of Spring Valley. Edna seemed to have made the transition from Canadian socialite to Midwestern farmer's wife with ease, as she was very popular with all her neighbors.

After a couple of months out of the ring, Billy became bored with farming, and at the age of twenty-four, he found it easy to get back into fighting shape. Billy started working out again in the local gyms when Ed broke the news to him that Australian promoters had lined up a series of fights for him if he was willing to return to the ring. His first opponent was to be Australian strong man Big Ed Williams. The temptation was too much for Billy to resist. He went home to talk to Edna about the tour. Edna agreed to the tour, only if she could go along with Billy and his brother.

Edna wired her parents to tell them that she would be going on tour with Billy on a trip to Australia and then onto England. The young wife was very excited as she shopped for the trip while Ed, who was now acting as Billy's manager, made all the financial arrangements.

Billy was in top shape and hoped to eventually lure Stanley Ketchel back into the ring to finally decide in his mind who the better man was in the ring.

The young wife was very excited to be going on her first international trip and could not have been more in love with her young, handsome, blond husband. She did not want to see Billy get hurt in the ring, but fighting appeared to make him happy, and she saw that he was certainly good at it. Edna liked all the fame and attention that Billy brought upon them, and although she missed her family, she did not miss her old lifestyle at all.

Even though the Papkes made a handsome couple, they had come from entirely different backgrounds. Billy's family came from a strict German, male-dominated, blue-collar family, while Edna was born into wealth due to her father's manufacturing business. The difference in backgrounds would certainly come into play some twenty-five years later.

World Tour

IN SEPTEMBER OF 1910, the Papke clan set sail for Australia and were met by a friendly press, unlike the hostile press that Billy had encountered in France in March. Just ten days before his scheduled match with Ed Williams on October 25th, news coming from the United States reported that Middleweight Champion Stanley Ketchel had been shot and killed in Conway, Missouri, by a jealous farmhand named Walter Dipley. Ketchel had developed a reputation as quite a womanizer, and apparently Dipley felt that Ketchel had made improper advances towards his fiancee.

No matter what the circumstances were, the fact remained that Billy Papke was never going to fight Stanley Ketchel again and prove that he was the better man in the ring.

The Australian promoters seized on the opportunity of Ketchel's death to now advertise the Papke-Williams fight-to-be for the Australian version of the vacant middleweight title. Billy was both angry and upset with the news of Ketchel's death.

Billy stepped into the ring in Sydney with the sole purpose of showing the world that he now was undoubtedly the best middleweight in the world. He came out charging at the sound of the first bell against Williams and clobbered him with his entire arsenal until he dropped him hard to the canvas in the fifth round with a hard right cross. Williams made up for his lack of skill with gameness and toughness. He was able to withstand Billy's assault and made it through the fifth round. Billy's attack was nonstop in the sixth round, and he dropped Williams twice more with vicious uppercuts. Williams wobbled back to his corner, but his corner threw in the towel before the start of the seventh round. Billy was now champion of the world again, at least as far as Australians were concerned.

It was quite a day for Billy, as Edna advised him when he got home that she was pregnant with their first child. Billy could not have been happier, and the Australian press followed the couple everywhere. Billy's picture was on the sports pages on a regular basis. He had relatives on his father's side visit in Sydney, and they found Edna to be very pretty and charming.

Billy celebrated the following Christmas a little too much, and he took on the undefeated Dave Smith the day after Christmas. Billy looked slow and out of shape and was disqualified in the tenth round for one too many violations. He kept his title, but he seemed to lack motivation in this fight.

On February 11, 1911, Billy defended his claim to the title against Cyclone Johnny Thompson in Sydney. Thompson was a crafty veteran who stood only five foot four. Thompson, like Billy, was also from Illinois, and he had a slick hit-and-run style of boxing. Both fighters entered the ring in top shape. Billy always had trouble with boxers who moved around the ring a lot, and this fight was no exception. Billy appeared unscathed after the contest, but he was unable to catch Thompson with any solid punches, and he lost his title on a unanimous decision to the veteran fighter.

Billy took the loss philosophically and returned to the ring the following month to take on the undefeated Dave Smith in a rematch. Billy looked like a sure loser again after six rounds of fighting but came alive in the seventh round to knock Smith down twice. The fight was stopped, and Billy was declared the winner in his final fight in Australia.

Leaving on a high note, the Papke clan said good-bye to Australia and set sail for merry old England. The middleweight title was again declared vacant as Johnny Thompson gave up his claim as champion due to weight making problems. When Billy arrived in England, he was signed to fight local tough man Jim Sullivan. This time, the British promoters declared this bout for their version of the vacant middleweight title due to Thompson giving up his claim.

The fight was scheduled for June 8th at the Palladium in London. Five days before the fight on June 3rd, Edna gave birth to Billy Papke Junior, the couple's first child.

When Billy entered the ring at the Palladium, he had another mouth to feed, and he was very motivated to win. The bout was scheduled for twenty rounds and had been highly publicized in the local media. The sold out Palladium was hoping for a British middleweight champion when Billy showed up in the ring wearing boxing shorts instead of his customary jockstrap. The British fans applauded both fighters politely when they entered the Palladium ring. Sullivan, unlike Ed Williams in Australia, was a fast-moving boxer who had a lot of finesse but did not have much of a punch. Sullivan tried to hold Billy off with his jab, but Billy ripped vicious uppercuts to the chin in the infighting and ripped him with left hooks and right crosses to the jaw at long range. Billy was careful not to hit below the belt as the British were known to be very quick to disqualify American fighters for excessive body punching.

Billy pounded Sullivan's head and body in every round, and the crowd was hollering at the referee to stop the contest in the ninth round. Sullivan's face was a bloody mess, and he had suffered several cracked ribs during the contest. The crowd cheered when Billy's hand was raised in victory in the middle of the round by the referee. Billy had at separate times won French, Australian, and British support as champion, but universal recognition as champion had thus far eluded him.

Billy cut his celebration short in England, as Edna wished to return home with their infant son. The trip had been very lucrative for the Papkes, as Billy had picked up two more versions of the middleweight title, and added income. The Papkes could not have been happier when they sailed back to America.

Billy arrived home and adjusted back to farm life as Edna became a stay-at-home mother with Billy Junior. Billy always led a frugal lifestyle and never cared much for the nightlife as did Stanley Ketchel. Due to his lifestyle, he was never as popular with the press as Ketchel was. Billy had a spacious house on Roosevelt Avenue and had other real estate in Kewanee besides his chicken farm.

Billy Junior was a healthy blond-haired boy like his father; Billy spent a great deal of time at home helping Edna to raise their son. One summer night, his brother Ed came over to their house to tell Billy that he had been scheduled to defend his title against Sailor Burke in New York in August. Billy had already won a newspaper decision over Burke in August of 1908, just prior to winning the middleweight title from Ketchel.

On August 22nd, a very confident Billy Papke stepped into the St. Nicholas arena in New York to face Burke. In New York at the time, no official decisions were allowed, and a fighter could only lose his title by knockout. It was this rule that saved the title for Billy as he was pummeled around the ring for all ten rounds to lose in an unofficial newspaper decision.

Two months later in Boston, Billy lost another ten-round decision, this time to Bob Moha in an over-the-weight nontitle match. Billy celebrated Christmas with his family and then dropped his third straight over-the-weight match to Frank Mantell in February in Sacramento,

California. Billy finally returned to his winning ways by knocking out Billy Leitch in New York on May 2nd.

French boxing promoters contacted Ed Papke to set up a series of title matches for Billy in France. It appeared that Billy needed to travel to find any motivation for him to achieve any real success as champion. French promoters wanted him to defend his title against rising French star Marcel Moreau on June 29th in Paris. Billy jumped at the opportunity to make the title defense, but this was not to be the start of a tour as Edna was staying home with Billy Junior.

Billy entered the Cirque de Paris ring on June 29th, to defend his title against the French star. The French press apparently had forgiven him for his previous altercation that occurred before the Willie Lewis fight two years earlier. The fans cheered when Moreau entered the ring. The French fans had even more to cheer about when Moreau dropped Billy in the very first round and nearly knocked him out. Billy defended himself well in the next couple of rounds and actually dropped Moreau to the canvas in the eighth round with a straight right hand. Billy kept working Moreau's body and was taking command of the fight. Moreau suffered a terrible beating in the fifteenth round and had to be carried back to his corner. Before the start of the sixteenth round, Moreau's corner threw in the white towel of surrender, and Billy had successfully defended his title once again. Billy was really becoming a road warrior and did his best fighting on foreign soil. The French press had really warmed up to Billy, and he was on his best behavior on this trip. He sailed home with his title intact and a large sum of French money.

Billy and Ed arrived in Kewanee and spent the summer of 1912 at home with their families in Kewanee. Ed had opened up a United Cigar Store in town and Billy was busy taking care of his farm and real estate investments. Billy could be seen in town touring around on a regular basis with his new Glide-type vehicle. The vehicle was a seven-seater and was more of a family vehicle than his old green Stutz roadster.

Who's the Champ?

BILLY RETURNED TO St. Nicholas arena and fought a ten-round, no-decision match with Jack Denning in New York on September 25th, and two days later, fought a six-round, no-decision match with Leo Houck in Philadelphia in a wild slug-fest. Newspaper articles at the time wrote that the Houck corner claimed that Billy was using sliced up gloves for the contest. The referee examined the gloves and made Billy put on a different pair before the fight started. Billy became incensed and went after one of Houck's corner men who was hollering at him during the fight. At one point, Billy got knocked out of the ring and climbed back in and head butted Houck, according to the newspaper accounts. Houck was the hometown fighter and was given a Philadelphia hometown newspaper decision over Papke. Billy had developed a habit of using these no-decision fights as tune-ups to his major title defense fights. Controversy seemed to follow Billy wherever he fought.

Billy returned to Paris with Ed on October 23rd to put his title on the line against French idol Georges Carpentier. The eighteen-year-old Carpentier had already had over seventy professional fights and figured to be a real challenge to Billy's title. Billy weighed in a couple of ounces over the middleweight limit at the time of 158 pounds. Then he weighed in nude and still could not make the weight. The

Carpentier camp refused to give Billy more time to shed the excess ounces, and Billy had to forfeit $2,500 to Carpentier. Billy was furious when he entered the ring to do battle and vowed to make Carpentier pay in blood for the forfeited money. The French fans were 100 percent behind Carpentier, and the Cirque de Paris was filled to overcapacity for this fight. The fight was scheduled for twenty rounds, and it was Billy's most important fight since his series with Stanley Ketchel.

The younger and faster Carpentier was expected to be too fast and slick for Billy, as it was known that Billy had a hard time with quick-moving boxers. Carpentier started out fast in the first few rounds, throwing lightning-like combinations and avoiding all of Billy's slow rushes. At the end of the fourth round, Billy began blinking and stated that he was blinded by a foreign substance on Carpentier's body. The referee examined Carpentier and found that he had some chemicals in his hair that had blinded Billy. Billy refused to win the fight by disqualification, and instead, was given five minutes to recuperate. By the eighth round, Billy's body punching began to slow down Carpentier, and the fight was now fought on even terms. Carpentier stayed competitive in the fight, even though he was absorbing a brutal body beating. Billy smiled throughout the fight, as he seemed to be enjoying his work. Carpentier staggered back to his corner at the end of the sixteenth round, but came out throwing desperate combinations in the seventeenth round until he suffered a huge cut over his right eye. Billy went after the cut and was pounding Carpentier all over the ring when the bell rang. Carpentier was literally out on his feet and was unable to come out for the eighteenth round. Billy had defeated another French hero, and this was his biggest victory since he had defeated Stanley Ketchel in 1908 for the title. It should be remembered that this was the same Georges Carpentier who went on to win the light heavyweight title, and then stun Jack Dempsey with a right-hand punch in their heavyweight title fight.

If not universally recognized as champion, the consensus of the fight public considered Billy as the middleweight with the best claim to the title. The popular Papke stayed in Paris with Ed, and another fight was scheduled for Billy to defend his title. The new opponent would be Georges Bernard, and the fight was set for December 4th in the same ring where he had defeated Carpentier. Billy knew little about Bernard except that the French press were labeling him as the "French Killer" for devouring all of the French fighters put in front of him.

Bernard would fare no better than Carpentier, as he was beat so badly that he could not come out of his corner for the seventh round. Papke was hailed as invincible by the French press. Billy had beat all of the French fighters put in front of him. It was time for him to head home for Christmas. Sailing across the ocean was becoming a regular routine for the Papke brothers, and it was hard on a young wife to stay at home with a young child.

Billy and Ed spent Christmas at home with their families. Ed tended to his cigar store and Billy to his real estate investments. Billy Junior was growing up fast now, and Billy had not had a chance to spend a lot of time with him. All of Billy's tough fights and world tours were starting to catch up to him. Even though he was now only twenty-six years of age, he had fought professionally for eight years and was beginning to tire of fighting. Billy thought that a champion should lose his title in the ring and not just give it up. He agreed to return to Paris for one last time to defend his title against Frank Klaus of Pittsburgh.

Billy had already lost a newspaper decision to Klaus, and their return match was set for March 5, 1913, in the Cirque de Paris. Billy fought one of his most undisciplined fights of his career. He continually punched Klaus low until the referee had no choice but to disqualify Billy in the fifteenth round for continual fouling. After the fight, Papke had hardly a scratch on him, while Klaus was covered with bruises all over his face and body. This was the last significant fight of Billy's career.

Billy returned to Kewanee without the title and worn out from all the years of ring battles and traveling. He had been a professional boxer since 1905, and his aggressive style of fighting was one style that did not lead to a long boxing career. Billy helped Ed out with his cigar store in his spare time and did try a minor comeback in October. He traveled to St. Louis, Missouri, and dropped an uninspired eight-round decision to some unknown fighter named Marty Rowan. Billy had definitely lost his desire to continue fighting by this time.

By 1914, the war was raging in Europe. It was no longer a safe place to fight. Billy helped Ed run the cigar store business, and he had plenty to do in taking care of his real estate holdings and chicken ranch. The Papkes' second child named Clifford was born on March 15, 1914, and their third child, Robert, was born on October 8, 1915. Billy bought another house at the edge of town on Fischer Road. He was regarded as a respectable businessman in Kewanee. All the townspeople still called him champ. Billy Junior was attending the public school system in Kewanee, and Edna was taking care of the other two baby boys at home. Billy moved his parents to Kewanee with his ring earnings, and Edna's parents were frequent visitors to visit the children. Edna's father was always willing to give Billy advice on how to conduct his businesses. While initially being against the marriage, Edna's family adjusted well to their son-in-law.

While driving to visit Edna's parents in Canada, Billy stopped off in Brooklyn, New York, against Edna's wishes, to partake in a ten-round boxing exhibition against one Jack Smith. Billy did not fare well after being out of the ring for close to four years, and he lost a newspaper decision. The Papkes returned to Kewanee, where Billy had to register for the draft. He received a deferment from the military due to the fact that he had a wife and three children by this time. He listed his occupation as farmer, and though he was of German descent, he was a citizen by birth and local sports legend, thus avoiding much of the animosity against Germans during the war. At this time, German language classes were discontinued from the public school system in Kewanee, and Germans who were not yet citizens were taken to relocation camps, which included Texas.

Billy had fought frequently in California and liked the mild climate and sunny weather. Edna had been to California on several occasions with Billy during his fights and also liked the West Coast atmosphere. Billy and Ed saw great real estate potential on the West Coast and began making long-range plans for the cross-country move. Billy's body was worn out from all of his fights, and his championship days were most certainly over.

After defeating Ketchel for the title, Billy had received some offers in California to go into acting. His loss to Ketchel two months later in the rematch killed all hopes of an acting career, and the defeat caused him a severe loss of potential income. Billy was still popular on the West Coast, as his title fights with Ketchel were considered ring classics. His fourth fight with Ketchel in 1909 had been filmed and had been played in all the theater houses of the time. During the early 1900s, the middleweight championship of the world was nearly as prestigious as being the heavyweight champion.

The Papkes decided to keep the cigar store in Kewanee in the family, and Billy and Ed and their wives were planning on making the move to California. Billy especially liked the Southern California area the best. He saw great potential for buying acreage in the undeveloped areas around Los Angeles County. It finally became time for the Papkes to say good-bye to Midwest living.

California, Here I Come

BY 1918, WORLD War I was coming to an end and the nation was returning to what was called the period of normalcy. The United States and their Allies were victorious in the war to end all wars, and the economy was beginning to grow again.

Billy Papke did not enter the war, as he was married and had three children by the time the United States became involved in the worldwide conflict. Billy's father, Edward, passed away suddenly in Spring Valley in 1918, leaving Billy's mother, Emma, a widow. In 1919, the Kewanee public records indicated that Billy and Ed Papke and their families no longer resided in Kewanee. While in California with the family, Billy boxed two exhibition matches. He boxed a four-round exhibition bout with Soldier Bartfield in April, and a four-round exhibition match with Jimmy Darcy in May, in San Diego.

After Billy's final exhibition match, he moved the entire family, including his mother, to Los Angeles County in Southern California. Billy was always looking for real estate, and he found it in the Los Angeles area. He immediately bought an orange ranch near Altadena, and a ten-acre citrus grove in a Los Angeles suburb named San Dimas, California. His boys were now being educated in the California school system. Billy's estimated worth, according to newspaper articles at the time, was $300,000, which would be equivalent to close to $4 million by 2015 standards.

Billy always found time to referee boxing matches and have his picture taken with boxing champions and movie stars. He was also an extra in Hollywood movies for a dozen years. Edna, who had been raised in a cold Canadian environment, found the sunny California weather just to her liking and adapted well to the social scene in Southern California. Ed and his family also moved to Southern California while maintaining their interest in the United Cigar Store in Kewanee.

The 1920s were called the roaring twenties by the press. The 1920s were a time of huge celebrations. Some of the famous people of the twenties were boxing champion Jack Dempsey, movie star Rudolph Valentino, and gangster Al Capone. The favorite dance was the Charleston, and Prohibition had come into being. Silent movies gave way to the talkies around 1927, and Babe Ruth was breaking home run records with the New York Yankees. The 1920s were also a time of women's liberation, which did not really set well in the conservative household of Billy Papke.

Bootleg whiskey could always be found if you knew which nightclub to attend, and Al Capone was making news with the St. Valentine's Day Massacre in Chicago. The middleweight boxing division, as always, was in a state of confusion as to who was the champ, and the sport was more popular than ever.

Billy once told the press that he had $100,000 in theatrical appearances lined up after he beat Stanley Ketchel for the title. The immediate loss of his title within two months caused his sponsors to back out of the proposal. Frugal as he was, Billy made his brother Ed his manager and trainer after the title loss to Ketchel. During the latter part of his career, he was managed, in part, by Sam Berger and Al Lippe. Lippe, like Jones before him, had many boxing connections with promoters, especially in Europe.

Billy Junior, the eldest of Billy's three boys, was sixteen years of age in 1927, and he was very athletic and blond like his father. Billy wanted to groom his oldest son to be a fighter and lead him to a world title. Times were definitely changing in the country, but Billy still ran his household as a male-dominated home. Edna had made new friends in Southern California and found the roaring twenties and liberated thirties to her liking. Edna, who had been raised in an affluent Canadian family, had to make the switch to small-town Midwestern housewife when she married Billy. After raising three sons, she enjoyed her newfound freedom in California. All three of the boys were doing well in school, and Billy was making a fortune in real estate around the San Dimas and the Pasadena area with his orange and fruit farms.

Billy never turned down an offer to referee a boxing match or have his photo taken with current boxers and movie stars. He liked to hang out with his old boxing pals, including old foe Fireman Jim Flynn and former heavyweight boxing champion Jim Jeffries. Billy divided much of his time running his farms and helping brother Ed with his cigar store in Kewanee. The mood of the country was of a party nature, with plenty of excesses. There was plenty of food, plenty of work, no war, and a great sense of freedom. The whole world was one big party, as the decade was winding to an end. Billy Junior turned eighteen in 1929 and was one year away from turning to a professional boxing career. Billy had hoped that his son would also claim another world boxing title for the family.

The Great Depression

THE COUNTRY WAS in a state of shock in October of 1929. The unthinkable had occurred as the bottom had fallen out of the stock market and wealthy people who had suddenly lost their fortunes were jumping out of windows. The Papkes, like most American families, were affected by the depression. Billy had grown up in hard times, but he had never seen such a change in the country's fortunes like what had occurred in 1929. The value of land prices dropped considerably, and many people were out of work. The poor economy caused many people to lose their jobs, homes, and farms. Billy had developed a shrewd business sense growing up in Kewanee, and he was able to ride out the depression without losing his farms.

People became very transient, and hobo jungles were found in all parts of the country. Soup kitchens were set up for people who were homeless and had no money for food. Wealthy people became poor people, and poor people became even poorer. Hobo jungles were called "Hoovervilles," named after the current president Herbert W. Hoover. Rightly or wrongly, Hoover was blamed for the bottom dropping out of the economy, and he was soundly beaten by Franklin D. Roosevelt in 1932 in a bid for presidential reelection.

Billy was now turning his attention to Billy Junior's boxing career. Billy Junior, who had been born in England, had grown into a solid

170-pound light heavyweight and bore a strong resemblance to Billy with his square face and light blond hair. Billy Junior turned professional at the age of nineteen in August of 1930 under his father's guidance. Billy Junior received a great deal of press coverage and fanfare being the son of a famous middleweight boxing champion. Billy Junior fought mostly in Hollywood and at the Olympic Auditorium in Los Angeles during his first year of fighting. He went undefeated in his first seven fights until he lost a decision to Jimmy Hanna in August of 1930.

Billy Junior sustained a broken jaw in a knockout loss to Billy Wagner in March of 1931 in Pasadena. His father thought a change of scenery might rejuvenate his son's boxing career, and he brought him back to Illinois to introduce him to the Kewanee fight fans in May of 1931. Billy and his son received much press coverage in the local newspapers, and it was written up how well Billy had done financially in California.

Billy's return to Illinois with his son made front sports page headlines as his son trained in Kewanee for his scheduled ten-round bout with Edgar Norman in June in Chicago. Billy advised the press that he felt in a couple of years under his guidance that his son would be ready for a shot at the light heavyweight title. Billy was training his son himself and managing all aspects of his boxing career. On June 11th, Billy Junior stepped into the ring in Chicago and lost a lopsided ten-round decision to Norman. It was later claimed that Billy Junior had not fully recovered from his broken jaw suffered in the March fight with Billy Wagner in California. Though Billy was a great fighter, it was written that he may have pushed his son too soon in trying to make him a champion.

Billy returned to California with his son in an effort to rebuild his boxing career. Billy Junior had moderate success in California rings in 1932, and then he was matched against a local Mexican fan favorite Bert Colima in January of 1933 in Pasadena. Billy Junior knocked out Colima in a wild first round that had the fans on the edge of their seats. Billy Junior had his father's power, but not his killer instinct.

In June of 1933, Billy Junior won the California State light heavyweight championship over Tom Patrick, earning him an over-the-weight match against Middleweight Champion Gorilla Jones. In September, Billy Junior entered the ring in Pasadena to face his stiffest test as a professional. He fought hard, but took a terrific beating and was stopped in the eighth round by Jones. This fight effectively ended Billy Junior's hopes of ever being a world-class fighter. He ended his career by winning a couple of decisions in four-round fights in 1934 at the Hollywood Legion Stadium.

Billy Junior, realizing that he was not championship material in the ring, eventually became a police officer in La Verne, California. He was a very good main event fighter, but the fact was that he was not of championship caliber like his father. This was not an unusual occurrence as in many cases, the son does not match the success made by a famous father. Billy had to accept the fact that there would be no more champion boxers in the family. In an interview in 2015 with Billy Junior's granddaughters Dayna Pacquette and Lisa Pardue, this author was advised that Billy Junior lacked the killer instinct to be a fighter and really never wanted to harm anyone.

Trouble in Paradise

THE 1930S BROUGHT many changes to the Papke household. Billy, for the first time in his life, was having a hard time finding new goals to achieve. His hopes of his son winning a world title had gone up in smoke, and the depression had affected his farm values. Billy became increasingly irritable and temperamental at home, and became insanely jealous of Edna's every move.

Billy was not aging well and changing with the times. With him being brought up in a strict male-dominated German household, and Edna in a more liberal, wealthy, Canadian environment, problems arose in the home. The couple had grown apart, and Billy felt lost in the modern world. Now that the boys were older, Edna wished to have more freedom to go out and visit her friends. Billy's fighting days were long since over, and Billy Junior was no longer boxing. The other two boys showed no interest in boxing. Billy's farming interests were not enough to keep him busy, and he spent more time at home and began to become increasingly jealous of Edna's every move. Edna, coming from an affluent Canadian family, had made many educated friends in Southern California. Billy, with his lack of formal education, always felt uncomfortable around her friends and eventually banned them from his household.

In time, Billy became even more jealous and began accusing Edna of imagined infidelities. Edna found it more and more difficult to live with him but stayed in the house and tried to save the marriage. All three of their boys were at least eighteen years of age and were moving out of the house. Edna had made many friends and had a large support system helping her in Southern California.

Billy's behavior around the house started to become erratic. He would throw temper tantrums on almost a daily basis, and Edna worried about his emotional and mental instability. She felt that Billy might be suffering from some sort of dementia due to the sixty-four tough professional fights that he had. There was no doubt that Billy's world was crumbling due his marital problems with Edna, Billy Junior's failure to become another boxing champion in the family, and his fight with depression or dementia. Billy was becoming disoriented to the point where Edna had a hard time staying under the same roof with him.

Edna was finally unable to cope with the stress of Billy's jealous tirades, and instead of celebrating her twenty-fifth wedding anniversary with him, she filed for divorce in the California courts in 1935. Billy was both stunned and irate at the divorce proceedings initiated by her. He did not want the divorce, but he could not change Edna's mind about proceeding with it. Billy did not wish to live alone. He moved in with his sons in the Los Angeles area after Edna's departure. Billy did not contest the divorce in court but began making threats if Edna did not reconcile with him. At the age of fifty, Billy had grown heavy and was a far cry from the man who had held the middleweight title until 1913. To make matters worse, Billy began drinking heavily and continued to beg Edna to reconcile with him. At this point, Edna had moved on with her life and allowed the divorce to become final in the early part of 1936.

Billy had met Edna in 1908 when he had acquired money and fame as a boxer. Edna had been raised in a wealthy family in Canada. Both of them were young and financially secure. By the 1930s, with the children out of the house and spending more time together, their cultural differences were glaring. Edna had undergone a change and felt a sense of freedom in California living in the 1920s. Billy had not adjusted to his life outside the ring as well as Edna and felt definitely lost with his boxing career over.

Unable to fight anymore, and with Edna gone, Billy traveled aimlessly around the Los Angeles area and spent time drinking and gambling in Las Vegas. He also developed the habit of taking up residence with his sons in the Los Angeles area at times, and he would continue to ask Edna, unsuccessfully, to reconcile with him.

New boxing fans did not remember the name Papke anymore. Stanley Ketchel had been gone since 1910, and the newspapers were full of stories of the new heavyweight sensation Joe Louis and current champion Jimmy Braddock. The middleweight division was muddled after champion Harry Greb's death in the 1920s, and, as always, several fighters were claiming the title, including Frenchman Marcel Thil. Old heavyweight champion Jack Johnson was all but forgotten in the press other than for a few scraps with the law.

The year 1936 did not present a bright future for Billy Papke. The country was still buried deep in the depression, and Billy Junior found employment as a policeman in the Los Angeles area, besides owning a landscaping company. Son Clifford became an agricultural researcher for a local company, and Robert became a plumber. They were living their own lives away from the boxing ring. Billy would occasionally visit the local gyms and swap tales with some of the older fighters that he knew from his ring days.

Murder and Suicide

BILLY'S DIVORCE HAD been made final in August of 1936, but in his mind, he felt that somehow he could get Edna to return to him. This may have been Billy's wishful thinking, and it is uncertain at this point how much his brain was affected by pugilistic dementia. Billy had certainly taken a severe beating in several fights, especially in the third Ketchel fight where he absorbed a tremendous amount of punishment.

In 1936, Billy had been living alternately with his sons Clifford in Los Angeles and Robert in Altadena, California. Edna had rented an apartment in the affluent Balboa Island section of Newport Beach, California, where she remained after Billy moved out in the preceding year. Billy called Edna frequently since the divorce had been made final the previous year and was becoming more and more agitated as his attempts of reconciliation were being consistently rebuffed.

During the summer of 1936, Billy became even more agitated with Edna's refusal of reconciliation and started making threatening statements to her. These statements escalated to the point where Billy threatened to do damage to both of them if she did not take him back. On one occasion, Billy threatened Edna with a gun, and his sons had to wrestle it away from him and unload the weapon. One must remember at this point that in the 1930s, domestic violence restraining orders were not in existence, and it is unclear why Edna did not take Billy's threats seriously.

Billy found employment in the summer of 1936 as a greeter at Jim Flynn's saloon in downtown Los Angeles. A sign in the window read: "Meet Billy Papke your host. Enjoy the simplicity and personality of a great champion." Billy took the job to help pass the time, which he hoped would take his mind off of Edna.

Billy's world began to crumble even more when, to add to his troubles, Stanley Ketchel's old trainer Pete "the Goat" Stone wrote an article in a national sports publication in October of 1936 where he claimed that Billy had only won the title because he punched Ketchel before the start of the second fight. Stone claimed that when Ketchel approached Papke at ring center to shake hands that Papke ignored the traditional gesture and punched Ketchel in the face with a two-punch combination that Ketchel never recovered from during the fight.

Many national sportswriters picked up on the story, and it became one of boxing's legends . . . that Papke had won the title in an, if not illegal manner, then certainly an unsportsmanlike manner. This article was devastating to Billy's reputation, and the story was generally accepted by the boxing public as being true, even though Stone had a reputation inside of boxing circles as being somewhat of an unstable personality. Stone had been Ketchel's trainer during the last portion of his career and was his sometimes drinking partner after the fights. When Ketchel was killed in 1910, Stone found himself unemployed, and by 1936, he was in desperate need of money. Stone was paid well by the magazine for his version of the fight events.

The holidays are always a sad time for people living alone separated from loved ones. Thanksgiving had never been a fond holiday of Billy Papke's. It was on Thanksgiving Day in 1908 when he lost his title to Stanley Ketchel and received a severe beating in the process. Billy had been especially morose while working at the saloon, often making statements like, "I just wish I knew what to do."

On the afternoon of Thanksgiving Day, the owner of the saloon, Ben Rosenberg, told Billy that he was going home to a turkey dinner. Billy replied, "I guess I will go too," and walked out of the building. Later in the afternoon, Billy called Edna on the telephone and advised her that he wished to drive to her residence and talk to her.

Billy arrived at Edna's home on Balboa Island, in Newport Beach, and walked to the front door. Edna, who was dressing to go out with a neighbor, walked to the front door to meet him. Billy advised Edna, "I have something to say to you, and it won't take very long. You won't have to get dressed." He then pulled out a .38 special caliber Colt revolver and slowly advanced toward Edna as she began backing away. Billy continued toward her, and then shot her once in the chest. As Edna turned to run away after being shot, Billy fired once more, and hit Edna in the back, thus, killing her. He immediately turned the gun on himself and shot himself three times in the chest. The last bullet pierced his heart. In a matter of moments, both Billy and Edna were dead near the front door of her residence.

The police arrived and spoke to the neighbor and friend of Edna's named Helen Cabbane. Mrs. Cabbane had planned on going out with Edna on Thanksgiving Day and called the police when Billy arrived at the residence and shot Edna and then himself. Mrs. Cabbane was in the house with Edna and saw Billy slowly advancing toward Edna with his gun and not saying a word to her prior to the shooting. She ran out of the house and immediately called the police after the first shot.

Mrs. Cabbane told the police that Billy asked if "Mommy was here" before he forced the front door open and shot Edna. She stated to the police that Billy had, several times, threatened to kill Edna, but Edna never reported this to the police as she often told her friends that

"Billy would never hurt me." Mrs. Cabbane also stated that Billy had frequently asked Edna to go back with him in the preceding months. According to her, Edna had finally stated that she would move out of the apartment the day after Thanksgiving and report the threats to the police department. The police advised local newspapers that the handgun used in the murder-suicide had been purchased by Billy approximately one week prior to this fateful Thanksgiving Day.

The shooting made front page newspaper headlines in the Los Angeles papers the next day. The headlines read: "PAPKE SLAYS EX-WIFE AND SELF, EX-CHAMP CARRIES OUT GUN THREAT." Several days later, Billy and Edna's children had the bodies of both parents cremated and buried together at a local cemetery in the Los Angeles area. Upon the reading of Billy's will, it showed that he owned a couple of farms in the Altadena area valued at a total of $20,000 and had $3,000 in cash. The amount of money left in Billy's will would be worth nearly $400,000 by 2015 standards, but still a far cry from the more than $300,000 in his bank account around 1920, which equaled close to $4 million by today's standards.

Billy had been described as an out of shape, lonely, middle-age man by the press in newspapers the following week. Comparisons were quickly made between the lives of Stanley Ketchel and Billy Papke. Both men were middleweight division world boxing champions who were born three days apart and came from the Midwest. Both men were no-holds-barred aggressive fighters, who never took a backward step. Both of them met violent ends, Ketchel by the hand of a jealous farmhand, and Papke by his own hand. It had been reported by previous writers that Ketchel and Papke died for the love of women; Ketchel, for the love of too many women, and Papke, for the love of one woman. Though Billy outlived Ketchel by some twenty-six years, they were not exactly considered peaceful years.

ROUND **Fourteen**

Victim or Villain?

WHEN THE NAME Billy Papke is mentioned, boxing fans usually think of two things. One, they think of the story where he supposedly sucker punched Ketchel before the start of their second fight. Because of this, the name Papke is often associated with ring treachery. The second thought is obviously the murder-suicide involving his ex-wife and himself, and the much-discussed circumstances of the killings. Let us now examine each event individually.

Did Billy Papke punch Stanley Ketchel in their second fight when Ketchel came to ring center to touch gloves before the bell? According to the Associated Press account of the second fight, Papke came out swinging at the bell and missed with a wild right hand. Ketchel actually landed the first punch of the fight, which was a light left hand to the face. During the first real exchange of the fight, Ketchel was stunned badly and dropped to the canvas.

Papke, after the fight, stated that he was not about to shake hands with Ketchel before the fight, as Ketchel immediately punched him when he went to shake hands with him before the first fight in Milwaukee. The local Illinois newspapers called this fight the "Milwaukee double cross." Ketchel himself never complained about being hit with a sucker punch before the start of the second fight. He merely advised the press that he was caught by surprise and should have been prepared. Ketchel vowed to avenge his defeat in the rematch.

The 1936 article of Pete "the Goat" Stone's account of the fight was published in all the boxing publications of the day and was handed down to future generations of boxing fans as gospel. In this sense, Papke was deemed a treacherous fighter by the boxing public, and he was the reason why future generations of fighters were made to shake hands before returning to their corners for the start of a fight.

The author prefers to believe the official Associated Press account of the fight, and that would mean that no such foul occurred at the beginning of the fight. Ketchel, as well as Papke, were both fighters who were willing to gain an edge at the beginning of a fight, if possible. It could be seen in fight number four, which was filmed, that both fighters are guilty of hitting during the break and elbowing each other. Both fighters were gladiators who never complained about their opponents' tactics.

What were the circumstances surrounding that fateful Thanksgiving Day in 1936? Billy Papke was a goal-oriented man. When he retired from fighting, he found no more goals to occupy his time. Billy had been an aggressive and violent man in the ring. Retired, he no longer had that physical outlet for that aggression. When Billy ended his boxing career, he was still in his late twenties, near the peak of his life physically. He was a restless man, who, for the first time in his life, had no goals. He had always been very much in love with Edna, but he also was always extremely jealous. When most of Billy's time had been occupied with his boxing career, this jealous trait had made their marriage difficult. Now that he was around the home much of the time, with little or nothing to do, his extreme jealousy made life for Edna impossible. Billy always felt out of place attending parties given by Edna's wealthy, college-educated friends. Billy claimed that Edna was flirtatious at the parties, and he quit attending them. He also wanted Edna to quit attending the parties without him.

Billy's hopes that his eldest son, Billy Junior, would blossom into a boxing champion and follow in his footsteps never materialized. Billy Junior had a winning boxing record, but he was unable to overcome world-class fighters.

There is also the distinct possibility with so many hard fights in the past that Billy may have been suffering from pugilistic dementia. Billy showed all the symptoms of this disease by acting totally disoriented weeks before the murder-suicide occurred. It would also be understandable to assume that he was wounded deeply by the accusations made by Ketchel's old trainer Pete Stone in an article published just one month before his death.

At the age of fifty, the old warrior appeared to be worn out, both physically and mentally. Papke stated frequently during the last two weeks before he died that he "just did not know what to do." It is unknown if his wild accusations of his wife Edna having affairs was true or not. Thanksgiving is a special time during the holidays for families to get together and celebrate. For Billy Papke, Thanksgiving was a curse. On this special day, he would lose his title and take a severe beating. During another Thanksgiving, he would take both Edna's and his life.

It would appear by statements made by Mrs. Cabbane, a neighbor, that Edna did not fear Billy and never thought that he would hurt her. It became obvious that Edna misjudged the seriousness of Billy's threats and mental state prior to the murder-suicide. It is impossible to tell what exactly was inside Billy's mind, but the fat and lonely middle-aged man who shot and killed Edna, before turning the gun on himself, was a far cry from the young dashing man that picked her up in 1910 and drove to Buffalo with her to get married.

After Papke's death, H. B. Murray, a former boxing manager and friend of Billy's, may have summed up the situation the best. Murray was quoted as saying, "Billy Papke was a one-woman man, and because he never loved, or even paid any attention to, any other women than his wife, he killed his wife, and then took his own life." Murray continued, "The same stubborn will which took him to heights in the prize ring made it impossible for him to accept defeat in his domestic affairs. He once told me after they separated, 'I'll get her back if I have to use a gun on both of us. She is not going to leave me, and no man is ever going to boast he took Billy Papke's wife to a dance.'"

Fifteen

A Final Tribute

WHY WAS STANLEY Ketchel so loved and Billy Papke so vilified? The answer could lie in their personalities. Stanley Ketchel loved the limelight and always had a great story for the press. Ketchel, like Jack Dempsey after him, started out life as a hobo who rode the rails throughout the Midwest in the early part of the twentieth century. Ketchel was a romantic figure during the early part of the century. He was a first-class womanizer and party animal. Like Babe Ruth after him, he would do everything to excess. He would fight forever, drink all night, and go for days with no sleep. Damon Runyon and other writers loved Ketchel and wrote about all his exploits, whether they were true or not. Other fighters read all about Ketchel as he died the only way they thought he would die—which was at the hand of a jealous husband or boyfriend. Ketchel did not care who he fought or who he made love with. At the age of twenty-four, he was dead and idolized by a generation of fighters and just about everybody in the fight game.

Billy Papke was pure fighter. As a young man, he worked hard in the coal mines and learned from his father how to be frugal with money. Though he liked flashy cars as a youth, he was never known to be a womanizer, and his father taught him how to invest his money. Whereas Ketchel was considered to be flashy, Billy was not. Billy saved his money, and by today's standards, he would have been considered a multimillionaire by the time he retired from the ring. He invested wisely in real estate in Kewanee and in California before the depression.

Billy could have very easily been given the decision in the close fourth fight, and the series with Ketchel would have been tied at two fights apiece. Both fighters came out fast in the first round of their first and second fights to try to gain an advantage, but nothing was reported except Pete Stone's biased article criticizing Papke's alleged "foul" at the beginning of the second fight.

Another little-known fact about Papke was found by reading old articles regarding his fights. Stanley Ketchel would fight anybody, anything, or anywhere. Ketchel challenged heavyweight champion Jack Johnson and actually dropped him before being knocked out in their title fight. Ketchel was willing to fight black fighters of his day, namely Jack Johnson, and middleweight Sam Langford. According to old press reports, Papke drew the color line and never fought a black fighter. It is unknown if this was Papke's idea or his manager, Tom Jones's. It was Tom Jones who advised the press that Billy would not defend his title against a black fighter after he had defeated Ketchel.

In 1972, Billy Papke was inducted into the Ring Magazine Hall of Fame and was rated among the top ten middleweight champions of all time by Ring magazine publisher Nat Fleischer. Billy's feats in the ring were also finally recognized by the International Boxing Hall of Fame, and he was inducted into their Hall of Fame in 2001.

There is no doubt that based upon his skill that Papke deserved to be in the Hall of Fame, and that his past reputation of treachery in the ring, unfounded or founded, delayed his induction, along with the sad ending of his and his wife's life. Billy Papke was a hard man, who grew up in hard times. He was a world champion boxer and a successful businessman in his lifetime. He traveled the world and was famous throughout the world in the sport of boxing. He was a wealthy man, but in the end, the possible dementia, unjustified negative publicity, and stubbornness of being unable to accept a failed marriage, were too much for the lonely old boxer to overcome.

Billy Papke was probably the most misunderstood of all the middleweight champions. Everything he did was newsworthy, from the way he won the middleweight title to the sad reports of the end of his and Edna's life.

I was able to locate one family member who actually met and talked to Billy Papke. John Widener is eighty-five years old and now lives alone in Oklahoma. John's mother was married to Billy Papke Junior. John remembers meeting the old middleweight champion on two occasions as a young boy. John tells me that Billy was very polite to him. He also remembers meeting Edna. John described Edna as a very quiet, well dressed, and cultured woman. John also said that Billy Junior rarely spoke of his father and the circumstances of the murder-suicide. Billy Papke Junior's granddaughter, Lisa Pardue, also informed me that because of the circumstances of the murder-suicide, her family did not celebrate the Thanksgiving holiday until around the late 1990s. Nann Papke Glauser was a great-niece to Billy Papke, and Ms. Glauser explained to this author that she could not recall her grandfather Fred, who was Billy Papke's brother, ever speaking of the great fighter. Fred Papke was the one brother who Billy had who did not move to California, but instead, stayed in Peru, Illinois. There was no doubt that the end of Billy Papke's life ended in a dark cloud that affected future generations of his family.

Billy Papke's life came to an end on that Thanksgiving Day in 1936, but his mind had been lost in another world years before the final tragedy of his life on earth. The inner desire and animal instinct that made great fighters out of men such as Stanley Ketchel and Billy Papke did not prepare them for the long run in the race called life.

Acknowledgments:

The following individuals were instrumental in helping me put this book together. I wish to thank all of them for their time and patience.

Larry Lock: President of the Kewanee, Illinois, Historical Society

Debb Ladgenski: Director of the Spring Valley, Illinois, Historic Association Board

Carol McGee: Bureau County, Illinois, Genealogical Society

Ian Wheeler: Orange County, California, Register Newspaper

Dayna Pacquette: Granddaughter of Billy Papke Junior

Lisa Pardue: Granddaughter of Billy Papke Junior

John Widener: Stepson of Billy Papke Junior

Nann Papke Glauser: Great-niece to Billy Papke

Dean Lingenfelter: Technical Support and Morale Booster

About the Author

The author Larry Carli, is a retired Sheriff Detective, and District Attorney Criminal Investigator from Sacramento County, California.

The author has a Bachelor of Arts Degree in Corrections from the University of California at Chico, and a Masters Degree in Criminal Justice from the University of Alabama.

The author has also written a cover story for Boxing Illustrated magazine,, as well as free-lance stories for Fight Beat and The Ring magazines.

The author currently resides in Elk Grove, California, and Rio de Janeiro, Brazil.

CPSIA information can be obtained
at www.ICGtesting.com
Printed in the USA
FSOW04n0125010717
35812FS